Contents

Clothes and Climate

There are many reasons why humans wear clothes. Some people like to 'dress up'. They feel good because they know that their clothes make them look attractive. Others may wear clothes to display their personality; to show what they do, or what special organization they belong to, such as the scouts or guides. But nearly everywhere

Brazilians have an opportunity to dress up in exotic clothes during 'Carnival', the yearly festival held in Rio de Janeiro.

COSTUMES
and CLOTHES

JEAN COOKE

Wayland

Topics

The Age of the Dinosaurs
Airports
Ancient Peoples
Archaeology
Bridges
Castles
Costumes and Clothes
Earthquakes and Volcanoes
Energy
Farm Animals
Great Disasters
Houses and Homes
Inventions

Jungles
Maps and Globes
Peoples of the World
Photography
Pollution and Conservation
Religions
Robots
Shops
Spacecraft
Stamps
Television
Trees of the World
Under the Ground

All the words that appear
in **bold** are explained in the
glossary on page 30.

First published in 1986 by
Wayland (Publishers) Ltd
61 Western Road, Hove
East Sussex BN3 1JD, England

© Copyright 1986 Wayland (Publishers) Ltd

British Library Cataloguing in Publication Data
Cooke, Jean
    Costumes and clothes. – (Topics)
    1. Clothing and dress – History – Juvenile
    literature
    I. Title   II. Series
    646'.3'09   GT518
    ISBN 0–85078–826–9

Phototypeset by
Kalligraphics Ltd, Redhill, Surrey
Printed and bound in
Belgium by
Casterman S. A.

People who live in very cold climates, such as this Inuit hunter, have to wear warm clothes.

people need clothes to protect them from too much heat or cold, because unlike animals and birds, we do not have furry coats or feathers. The clothes people wear depend on the climate of the area where they live.

People living in cold places, such as the **Inuit** of North America or the **Chukchi** in north-eastern Siberia, need thick clothes to keep them warm. However, some people are more used to the cold than others. When, in 1831, the scientist Charles

In warm, tropical climates it is more practical and comfortable for people to wear little clothing.

Darwin visited Tierra del Fuego, the island at the southern tip of South America, he found that the people living there wore nothing. Although the island is cool in summer and cold in winter, with biting winds, rain and sleet, their bodies had become adapted to the climate and clothing would have been impractical. Darwin and his British colleagues, however, were very glad of their warm clothes, which they were used to wearing in their own cold climate.

It is not surprising that in the tropics, the very hot lands that lie either side of the Equator, many people need very little clothing. Yet the Arabs and Berbers who live in the hot dry lands of northern Africa and south-western Asia wear loose robes that cover them almost completely.

In these desert regions the days are very hot indeed, and there is little shelter. Their long flowing robes help to keep the heat out. White robes are most suitable because white reflects the sun's rays and helps to keep them cool in daytime. The Arabs are glad of their robes at night, too, because after dark the temperature may drop to freezing point.

Europe and North America have hot summers and cold winters. People who live in these countries wear a style of clothing suited to the climate, which is often known as 'Western dress'.

People who live in very hot desert regions wear long flowing robes which keep the heat out.

Clothes and Fashion

For thousands of years rich people, who could afford to have lots of clothes made for them, adopted the latest styles in their efforts to look different from other people. Kings and other rulers have always wanted their clothes to be better than those of the people they governed. In Europe in the Middle Ages, laws, known as sumptuary laws, were passed. These stated what people might wear.

About the time of the Norman Conquest of England (eleventh century) men wore belted **tunics** and **breeches**. Working women wore an ankle-length tunic or dress, loose and unbelted with wide sleeves. Wealthier women wore a long under-tunic with a shorter one over the top.

In the 1500s European fashions were influenced by Spanish ideas. Men wore doublets, close-fitting

During the Middle Ages men wore tunics and tights and women wore loose, ankle-length dresses with wide sleeves.

By the sixteenth century, men were wearing shirts with big pleated collars called ruffs, and women wore uncomfortable corsets which made their waists look tiny.

jackets with very short sleeves, and short cloaks hanging from the shoulders. Over their hose they wore trunk hose, which were short, baggy knickerbockers, fitting closely round the thighs. Shirts had big pleated collars called ruffs. Women wore ruffs and uncomfortable corsets which made their waists look tiny. Their dresses billowed out over **farthingales**, which were bell-shaped underskirts made of canvas stiffened with hoops of cane.

In the 1600s fashionable men wore their hair long, and covered their coats in ribbons and lace.

In the 1600s fashionable men covered their knee-length breeches and coats with lace and ribbons, and wore their hair long. Women generally dressed more plainly than men.

During the 1700s and early 1800s a fashionable man's clothing was designed to make the wearer look slim and elegant. Men also wore long, curly-haired wigs. Women's clothes gradually became narrower, and under the influence of the French Empress Josephine, who favoured the style of the ancient Greeks, dresses became lighter with very high waists.

Throughout most of the 1800s the main garment for men was the frock coat, which fell to below the knee. Breeches became longer and were called pantaloons, and these in turn gradually developed into modern trousers. The lounge suit that men wear today was invented in the 1890s, but was only worn for informal occasions.

In the 1800s fashions were not usually as dramatic as this, though people did like to wear exotic headdresses.

In the late 1800s it was fashionable for women to wear a bustle, a padded cushion tied behind the waist under the dress to puff it out behind.

Women's clothes changed more rapidly. From the slim dresses of the early 1800s, they adopted the **crinoline**, which was something like the farthingale. This wired metal cage, worn with many petticoats, made the skirt billow out so that it took up a lot of room. The crinoline was so difficult to manage – it got caught up on furniture and in doorways – that it remained fashionable for only about twenty years. Its place was taken by the **bustle**, a padded cushion tied behind the waist under the dress to puff it out behind.

Men's clothing changed slowly in the 1900s towards what it is today. Women found that their long flowing skirts were no longer practical when they began to take over many jobs normally done by men. Skirts, which had risen to just

After the First World War women began to wear shorter skirts.

Miniskirts became fashionable in the 1960s.

above the ankles before the First World War, soared almost to the knee in the 1920s, and have stayed short for everyday wear ever since. The biggest recent change was the miniskirt of the 1960s, worn well above the knee.

Clothes experienced a virtual 'revolution' in the 1970s, when 'punk rock' became fashionable. Young people dyed their hair all sorts of different colours, and wore clothes made from plastic and even old rags. Some famous fashion designers used safety pins and other unusual materials to make their 'model' clothes.

Children's clothes are now much more practical than in former times, when even babies had to wear tiny versions of adult fashion. If their mothers wore a lot of petticoats and ruffles, little girls had to do so too. Little boys were dressed like their fathers, in clothes that were difficult to run about in and keep clean.

Interestingly, certain garments that started as underwear later became outer clothing. A shirt used to be worn under a tunic, but gradually more of it showed until today we think of it as the top layer in warm weather. Breeches for women, once considered very daring and never mentioned in polite society, have now emerged as shorts and trousers. Corsets and brassieres, which were never spoken of at all, are now worn as bathing suits and bikinis.

Clothes experienced a virtual 'revolution' in the 1970s, when 'punk rock' became fashionable.

Clothes and Work

People in every country wear clothes which are suited to their climate. Working clothes must obviously suit the type of job people do, but the climate has to be considered too. It would be impractical to wear heavy overalls it you live in a very hot country. In the West people wear clothes to show what they do and also to protect them from dirt or harm. Clothing that indicates what people do is generally known as **uniform**, a word which really means 'alike'.

The type of clothes we wear depends largely on the climate we live in. In a hot country like Brazil, it is more practical to wear shorts and short-sleeved shirts for work.

Uniform is so called because people doing the same job all wear the same kind of clothes. Policemen, soldiers, sailors, airmen and nurses all wear distinctive uniforms. Men and women such as doorkeepers, airline staff, bus drivers, security guards and post office and railway workers wear uniforms so that they can be easily identified.

Members of the police force wear distinctive uniforms.

Many industrial workers wear special clothing for protection. Miners, quarry workers, and people working on building sites wear hard hats to protect them from falling objects. In most factories people wear overalls to keep their ordinary clothes clean. Some workers wear shoes or boots with metal toecaps to protect their feet from injury.

Special clothing is designed to protect not only workers but also their products. This is particularly important when working with food, and with delicate devices like silicon chips.

Over the years some workers have developed distinctive clothing that is practical and has become almost a uniform. Cowboys in the American West wear close-fitting trousers, with leather **chaps** to protect their legs from thorns and branches. Their sombreros (wide-brimmed hats) keep the sun out of

People who work in certain industries have to wear special clothing, such as hard hats and gloves for protection.

American cowboys wear leather chaps to save their legs from thorns and branches, and wide-brimmed hats to keep the sun out of their eyes.

their eyes, and their high-heeled boots help to keep their feet in the **stirrups** when on horseback. The **gauchos**, the cowboys of South America, wear brightly coloured scarves and baggy trousers supported by wide silver belts.

19

Clothes and Religion

All through history, priests of many religions have worn special ceremonial garments for performing religious rites. When they carry out duties outside their places of worship many priests wear special clothes to indicate who they are. For instance, a Roman Catholic priest wears a long black gown called a cassock; Anglican clergymen wear a stiff white collar known as a clerical collar; a **rabbi** wears a tall hat and a long robe.

Catholic priests wear long gowns, like these, when performing certain religious ceremonies.

Many people wear clothes to show what religion they follow. Traditionally, the teaching of **Islam** requires that women wear long robes covering their bodies, and veils showing only their eyes.

Women still wear these traditional clothes in some Muslim countries, but in others they may wear Western dress. Muslim men who

Some women who follow the Islamic religion wear long robes covering their bodies, and veils showing only their eyes.

Buddhist monks from the Theravada *school wear long saffron robes. Those from the* Mahayana *school of Buddhism wear long red robes.*

have made the **pilgrimage** to Mecca, the holy city of Islam, often wear a green **turban**.

Orthodox (strict) Jewish men wear a small skullcap on the head, called a *yarmulkah*. Some also wear long sidecurls called ear-locks.

In the past, strict Christians known as Puritans believed that it was wrong to wear showy garments. They dressed in dull, dark clothes. Even today, some Christians, such as the Amish sect in North America, wear very plain clothes. Amish men wear black suits and wide-brimmed hats; the women wear plain, long dresses and bonnets.

The Amish people of North America wear very plain clothes.

Devout followers of the Sikh religion do not cut their hair. Sikh men are expected to wear a turban, and although in India boys do not usually wear one until they become adults, in Western countries, such as Britain, Sikh schoolboys often wear a turban to indicate their religion.

At Sikh weddings the bride and groom dress up in decorative and colourful clothes.

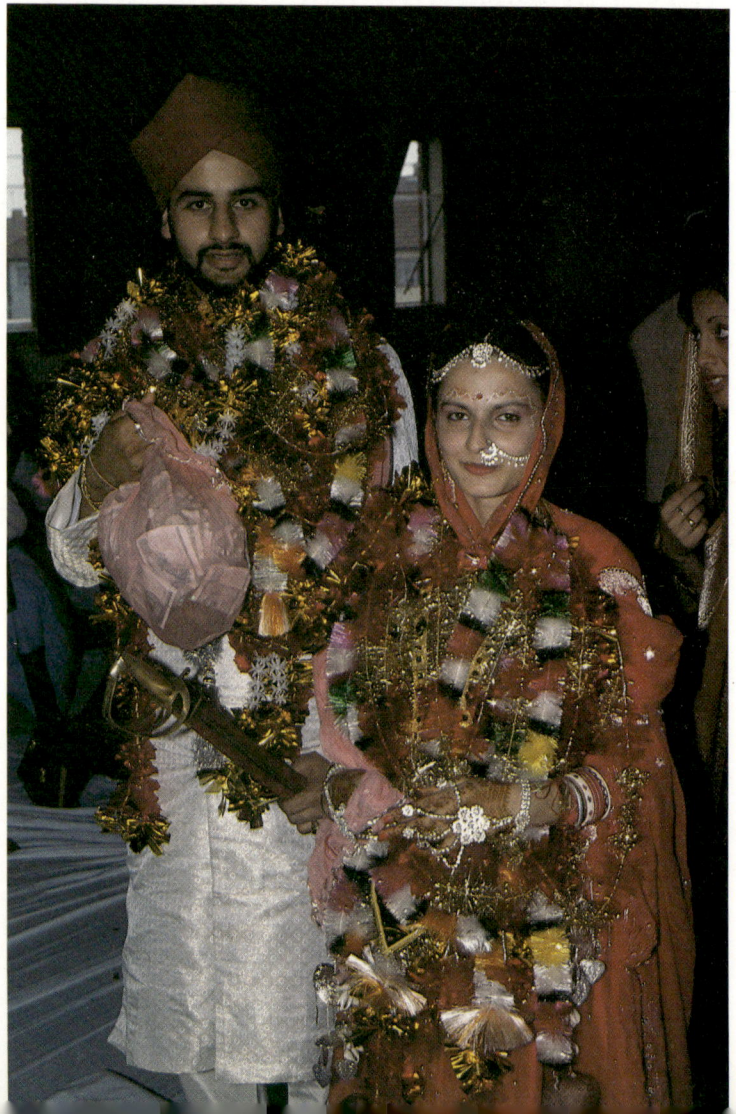

Clothes and Tradition

Tradition plays a large part in deciding what clothes we wear. In the Western world it has been the custom for many years for men to wear trousers and women to wear skirts. When women did begin to wear breeches as undergarments in the early nineteenth century, they borrowed the styles that men were wearing at the time. The only male skirts were the **kilts** of Scottish Highlanders and the kilted uniform of the *evzones*, the soldiers of the Royal Greek Guard.

In ancient times kilts were the standard dress for men in Egypt, Greece and Rome. Trousers were adopted from the tribespeople of northern Europe, who wore them for warmth in their cold climate. Turkish women, on the other hand, wore trousers. Today trousers are

A Scotsman wearing a traditional Highland kilt.

the normal wear for women in China and in many Muslim countries. In the Pacific islands men and women alike wear the *sarong*, a long skirt.

In India the traditional form of dress for men is a *dhoti*. This is a length of white material in cotton or silk. It is tied or wrapped around the body in various ways, according to the region. The usual form of dress for women is the *sari*, which is a very long strip of material swathed around the body. In parts of Africa too, men and women wear similar garments of brightly coloured cotton, which they wrap around their bodies. All these garments resemble the original Roman **toga**, which was also a long piece of cloth draped around the body.

Traditional costume survives for special occasions in most countries. Highlanders of Scotland wear their clan tartans and the kilt. Men of

The traditional form of dress for Indian women is the sari, *which is a long strip of material swathed around the body.*

Austria and Bavaria, in southern Germany, wear *lederhosen*, leather shorts held up by H-shaped braces, and the girls wear the *dirndlkleid,* consisting of an elaborately embroidered mid-length skirt and blouse. Many

Austrians in traditional costume.

Japanese relax at home in the *kimono*, a long robe tied with a sash. Trousers and tunics called *khameez* and *shalwar* are worn at Muslim and Sikh weddings.

Only a century ago most countries had their own traditional form of dress. Clothes continue to

A Japanese girl wearing a traditional kimono.

Lapp people continue to wear their traditional dress.

play an important part in the culture and heritage of people throughout the world. However, the everyday wearing of traditional costume is dying out in many countries, and more and more people are choosing to dress in 'Western' styles.

Glossary

Breeches Trousers reaching to the knee or just below.

Bustle A cushion, or metal or whalebone frame worn by women in the 19th century at the back below the waist to expand the skirt.

Chaps Overalls with no seat, worn by cowboys.

Chukchi One of many tribes living in the tundra regions of northern Europe and Siberia.

Crinoline A stiffened petticoat worn by women to widen skirts during the 19th century.

Farthingale A hoop or framework worn by women in Elizabethan times to spread their skirts.

Gaucho A South American cowboy.

Inuit The Eskimos of North America and Greenland.

Islam The religion of the Muslims, which teaches that there is one God and Muhammad is His prophet.

Kilt A knee-length, pleated skirt.

Pilgrimage A journey to a holy place as an act of religious devotion.

Rabbi The religious leader of a Jewish community.

Stirrup A horse-rider's foot support, attached to the saddle.

Toga An outer garment worn by the Romans.

Tunic A loose, sleeveless garment worn with trousers or a skirt.

Turban A man's headdress, worn by some Muslims and Hindus, and most Sikhs.

Uniform A set of clothes which show that the wearer belongs to a certain organization.

Books to Read

Costume Reference Volumes 1-9 (Roman Britain to 1950) by Marion Sichel (Batsford 1979).

Folk Costume of the British Isles by Lilla M. Fox (Chatto and Windus 1974).

Folk Costume of Western Europe by Lilla M. Fox (Chatto and Windus 1969).

Folk Costumes from Eastern Europe by Lilla M. Fox (Chatto and Windus 1977).

European Costume: 4000 years of fashion by Doreen Yarwood (Batsford 1974).

Hairstyles and Hairdressing by Molly Harrison (Ward Lock Educational 1968).

The History of Underclothes by C. Willett and Phyllis Cunnington (Faber and Faber 1981).

Picture Acknowledgements

Brian and Cherry Alexander 5, 29; Bruce Coleman Ltd 26; Mary Evans Picture Library 8, 9, 12, 13; Hutchison Library 7, 23, 24, 25; Marion and Tony Morrison *Cover*, 4, 16; Christine Osborne 21; Topham 14, 27; Wayland Picture Library, 6, 10, 11; Zefa 15, 17, 18, 19, 20, 22, 28

Index